Father Turk

Written by Peter Rees
Illustrated by John Bennett

Turkey

Contents

Who Was Atatürk?

Atatürk, whose full name was Mustafa Kemal Atatürk, is often called the founder of modern Turkey. A brilliant young army officer during World War I, Atatürk dedicated the rest of his life to working for peace, freedom, and equality for people in Turkey.

Before Atatürk, the lives of ordinary Turkish people had changed little for centuries. As the first president of the newly formed Republic of Turkey, Atatürk introduced widespread social and economic changes that improved the lives of most Turks. Even today, nearly 70 years after his death, his face appears on posters and billboards throughout Turkey.

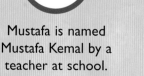

1881

Mustafa Kemal Atatürk is born simply "Mustafa" in Salonica, Macedonia.

1893

Mustafa is named Mustafa Kemal by a teacher at school.

1905

Mustafa Kemal graduates from officer school and is sent to train in Syria.

1915

Mustafa Kemal helps defend Gallipoli during World War I.

Setting the Scene

Turkey

For hundreds of years, the country we now call Turkey was part of the Ottoman Empire, which at its height stretched from North Africa to Asia and into parts of Europe. By the beginning of the 20th century, the Empire had shrunk greatly, as countries gained independence and left it.

The people of the Ottoman Empire were mostly poor farm workers and craftspeople. They were governed by a powerful ruler, called the sultan, who lived in Constantinople (now called Istanbul).

1919	1922	1923	1934	1938
Mustafa Kemal becomes the leader of the Turkish independence movement.	Mustafa Kemal defeats the Greek army at Dumlupinar in Anatolia.	Mustafa Kemal proclaims the new Republic of Turkey, with himself as president.	Mustafa Kemal takes the last name "Atatürk," meaning "Father of the Turks."	Mustafa Kemal Atatürk dies in Istanbul.

5

A New Name

1893

Mustafa's mathematics teacher glared at him, his bushy moustache twitching. Mustafa wondered why he had been called to his desk. He hoped he hadn't failed his homework assignment. Math was his best subject, and he was usually among the top in his class.

"There is a problem," the teacher began. "You see, your name is Mustafa. My name, too, is Mustafa. This won't do. Therefore, I have a new name for you." A smile appeared beneath the teacher's moustache. "Because you completed your homework assignment perfectly and then asked for more, from now on, you will be called Mustafa Kemal—Mustafa, the Perfect One!"

Mustafa Kemal was named just Mustafa when he was born in Salonica, in Macedonia. In those days, people born in some parts of the Ottoman Empire did not have last names.

Growing up, Mustafa was different from other boys. Unlike his friends, who all wore baggy oriental trousers, Mustafa preferred the Western-style uniforms worn by soldiers. As soon as he was old enough, Mustafa took the entrance examination for military school and passed.

Mustafa Kemal grew up in this house in Salonica (now Thessalonika) in Macedonia. Today, it is preserved as a museum.

Officer School

Mustafa Kemal studied the backgammon board. The situation looked hopeless. His opponent would certainly win in the next move. Mustafa Kemal frowned; he hated to lose.

At the next table, Ömer Naci, a classmate at the military college, was talking in a loud voice. "Why should the sultan have so much power?" he asked. "He hides in his palace, while his spies watch our every move. He suspends parliament and ignores the constitution. When will we Turks be allowed to govern our own country?" Others at the table agreed. Interested, Mustafa Kemal moved his chair closer to listen.

Mustafa Kemal moved to Manastir to attend military high school. There, he was introduced to politics through teachers and fellow students, such as the rebellious Ömer Naci.

At the time, it was dangerous to discuss ideas of freedom and equality. The Ottoman Empire was ruled by Sultan Abdul-Hamid II, who believed people could be governed only by force. He dissolved parliament and exiled or imprisoned many of his political opponents.

Sultan Abdul-Hamid II

In Syria

Captain Mustafa Kemal spurred his horse into a gallop across the sun-baked ground. He had been sent to train with the cavalry in Syria, which was part of the Ottoman Empire. The soldiers were looking for mountain tribespeople who refused to give up their independence and accept the sultan as their ruler.

This was a hard time for Mustafa Kemal. He had already made enemies among the cavalry officers because he opposed their practice of keeping gold that they found in the tribespeople's villages. Mustafa Kemal knew his fellow officers were paid poorly by the Ottoman government. But he also knew that theft and corruption were not the answers to their problems.

Mustafa Kemal was sent to Syria by the government because it suspected him of plotting against the sultan. Before long, however, he was organizing political meetings in Damascus while making plans to return home.

In 1906, Mustafa Kemal secretly traveled back to Salonica aboard a Greek ship. There, he met with others who wanted to help bring democracy to the Empire. After a few months, he was detected by the sultan's spies, so he returned to Syria to complete his army training.

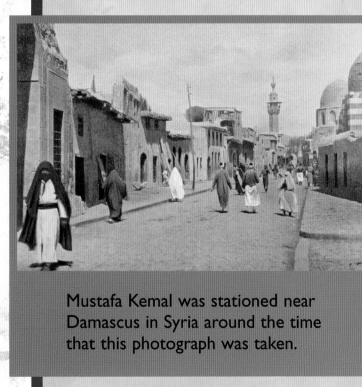

Mustafa Kemal was stationed near Damascus in Syria around the time that this photograph was taken.

The Young Turks

Salonica was celebrating. A group of army officers known as the Young Turks had overthrown the sultan's government and restored the constitution. People of different nationalities put aside their differences and embraced in the streets.

Celebrating with friends at a café, Mustafa Kemal wished he had returned from Syria earlier. His role in the revolution was small, and he did not like or trust all of its leaders. Still, he was determined to play a part in building a modern Turkey.

"One day you will be prime minister," he told a friend.

"And what will you be?" the friend asked.

"The man who appoints prime ministers!" Mustafa Kemal replied.

The celebration in Salonica didn't last long. Fighting soon broke out between different nationalities within the empire. To maintain control, harsh laws were passed, and the new government was soon as unpopular as the last one.

Taking advantage of the situation, neighboring countries invaded parts of the Ottoman Empire. Muslim refugees flooded into Istanbul to escape the conflict. Even Salonica was captured by Greece without a shot being fired.

Enver Pasha (1881–1922) was the leader of the Young Turks and a political rival of Mustafa Kemal.

refugee   a person who leaves his or her home because it is unsafe

13

Gallipoli

Chunuk
Bair •

Gallipoli
peninsula

Colonel Mustafa Kemal heard bullets whizz past and felt
explosions shake the ground. Enemy troops were firing
from a nearby hill called Chunuk Bair. If the troops weren't
forced back, they could capture the whole Gallipoli
peninsula and then march on Istanbul.

Mustafa Kemal had doubted whether the Ottoman Empire
should enter the World War on the side of Germany.
However, he would do anything to save his country from
being invaded. With a yell, he led his men up the hill.
As they neared the top, the enemy soldiers began to turn
and run. Suddenly, Mustafa Kemal felt himself knocked
backward. He reached into his pocket and removed
a shattered watch. The watch had stopped a piece of
shrapnel and saved his life!

peninsula   a narrow strip of land that
            juts into a sea or lake

Black Sea

Istanbul

Sea of Marmara

During World War I (1914–1918), the Ottoman Empire fought alongside Germany. The new government believed that Germany would win and help it regain territory lost in earlier wars.

However, Germany was defeated, and the Ottoman army was forced into retreat. Soon afterward, British troops occupied Istanbul. It was the end of the Ottoman Empire. Many of the Young Turks who had seized power fled the country, and government returned to the hands of the sultan and his supporters.

Around 325,000 Ottoman soldiers died in World War I, and many more were wounded. The number of civilian dead was even higher.

Ankara

1919

Three open-top cars wound their way across snow-covered mountains and vast *steppes*. From one of the cars, Mustafa Kemal could see the ancient walled city of Ankara below. Ankara had been home to Turks for centuries. From now on, it would be Mustafa Kemal's home.

After his brave leadership at Gallipoli, Mustafa Kemal had been hailed as a hero and given the title of Pasha, which means "Commander." However, he resigned from the army in anger over the government's decision to allow foreign troops to occupy parts of the country. He turned to politics and became the leader of a political organization that aimed to create an independent state for the Turkish people.

steppe   a large, treeless plain

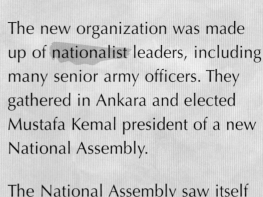

The new organization was made up of nationalist leaders, including many senior army officers. They gathered in Ankara and elected Mustafa Kemal president of a new National Assembly.

The National Assembly saw itself as the true representative of the Turkish people. It announced its intention to form a new democratic nation to be called Turkey, a name Westerners had long used for the region. Before long, much of Turkey was controlled by nationalists.

The National Assembly building in Ankara in 1921

nationalist someone who is fiercely loyal to his or her country

17

Under Attack

As soldiers carrying guns and ammunition hurried past, Mustafa Kemal wondered if Turkey would ever know peace and security. Two years before, Turkish troops had stopped an Armenian invasion in the east of the country. Now, Greek forces had burst into central Turkey. Once more, Mustafa Kemal had been called to lead the defense of his country.

Boom! The thunder of Turkish artillery rolled across the valley between the two opposing armies. At the same time, Turkish cavalry swept around the rear to take the Greeks by surprise. Although the Greek soldiers were better armed and equipped than his own, Mustafa Kemal hoped the plan would work. The future of Turkey was at stake.

artillery   large guns operated by crews

Mustafa Kemal had a favorite saying: *"Peace at home, peace in the world."*

Beaten back by the Turks, the Greek army retreated from the town of Afyon to Dumlupinar, 30 miles away. Three days later, they were routed by the Turkish army under the command of Mustafa Kemal. As the defeated Greek troops fled toward the coast, they burned hundreds of villages and towns.

The Greek commanding officers surrendered to the Turks in early September 1922. Turkey's three-year War of Independence was over. It was time to begin building the new nation.

The port of Izmir was mostly destroyed by fire during the 1922 Greek retreat.

rout   to defeat utterly

A New Nation

"Long live the Republic!" The cry rang out from the National Assembly in Ankara. It was a proud moment for Mustafa Kemal as his proclamation of the new Republic of Turkey was loudly welcomed by all.

Under Mustafa Kemal's leadership, Turkey had come a long way. The sultan had been overthrown. The National Assembly was now the recognized government of Turkey, with Ankara its capital. Turkey's borders were safe, and the foreign troops that had occupied it since the end of World War I had been forced out. Turkey, with Mustafa Kemal as its elected president, was now ready to take its place among the nations of the world.

republic   a state in which power is held
              by elected representatives

20

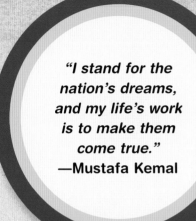

"I stand for the nation's dreams, and my life's work is to make them come true."
—Mustafa Kemal

On July 24, 1923, representatives of the Ankara government signed a peace treaty in Lausanne, Switzerland, with Greece and other countries, including Britain, France, and Italy. Under the Treaty of Lausanne, Turkey was recognized internationally as an independent state and regained land it had lost after World War I. In return, Turkey promised to protect the rights of minority groups.

The signing of the Treaty of Lausanne

The Speech

In October 1927, Mustafa Kemal gave a famous speech at a conference. It wasn't a short speech; it lasted for six whole days! In the speech, Mustafa Kemal described his life and the events that had led to the founding of Turkey. He urged the youth of Turkey to defend their country's independence at all costs, as he himself had done.

By the time he gave the speech, Mustafa Kemal was the dictator of Turkey. Dictators are often feared and hated in their own country. However, because of the reforms he made in education, religion, language, dress, and women's rights, Mustafa Kemal was revered in Turkey. He is now best known by the name he chose for himself in 1934: Atatürk. It means "Father of the Turks."

dictator a ruler who has complete power in a country

The Great Reformer

In Turkey, Mustafa Kemal Atatürk is sometimes called the Great Reformer. Reforming means changing something in order to improve it. Below are some of the many reforms Atatürk introduced to Turkey. Not all of them were popular at the time. Why do you think he made them?

- He simplified written Turkish and introduced the Latin (Western) alphabet and numbers in place of Arabic.

- He made last names compulsory.

- He reduced the role of religion in society.

- He helped women obtain the right to vote.

- He outlawed the wearing of the fez, a traditional Turkish headwear, in favor of Western-style hats.

The so-called "Hat Law" of 1925 made it a crime to wear a fez in public.

What If?

Mustafa Kemal Atatürk once said that "only teachers can save nations." Mustafa Kemal respected teachers because he had been encouraged to form ideas and opinions by teachers at school. He said of one of his teachers, "He opened a new horizon before my eyes." If young Mustafa Kemal hadn't been encouraged in this way, do you think he would have become the leader of Turkey? Why or why not?

Great leaders often show great determination. Besides determination, what other qualities should a leader have?

Index

determination a drive to succeed